FIGHTING THE FOOD MONSTER

Content

1. The food monsters.
2. 5Cs.
3. Addiction.
4. Keep it visual.
5. Head game – focus – Never Say Never – **NEVER EVER EVER GIVE UP.**
6. Talk about it.
7. I'm losing weight today.
8. Weighting regularly.
9. Weekly rhythm.
10. Food and exercise, Rhythm.
11. The person you are / Superpower.
12. The Maintain Game.
13. On the soap box moment!!!!
14. The Big Guy.
15. Notes to self.

Introduction.

I've written this manual instead of a book as a manual is a set of instructions to operate or control something. A book you read once, a manual you use every day and keep going back to.

This manual is here to help you control your FOOD MONSTER, your inner voice to lose weight and get to where you want to be – which always needs to be healthy and balanced.

There are many, many ways, ideas, food and exercise regimes out there to lose weight, but one thing remains the same no matter how you choose to lose weight and that is the psychological and emotional journey, it needs to be a lifestyle change forever, not a fad or unsustainable – so pick very carefully.

This manual is also designed to run along side any of the present weight loss products, eating plans, regimes presently on the market, because the psychological journey remains the same.

It is advisable to read each section of this manual in order first then you can revisit whatever section you want, if not, simply – it won't work (This is the only piece of negativity in the manual) but it's true.

You will need to use your imagination during reading this manual – you'll get the idea as we go along. I've tried to keep this manual as to the point and simple as possible, and for this manual to speak to each and every one of you that reads it.

IT WORKED FOR ME

A Small Bit About ME – I've never been small till now

I have been big / large, whatever you want to call it, all my life and at my biggest I was 30st 4lbs (427lbs, 193.6Kgs).

I hit the weight I wanted to be in October 2017 at 15st (210lbs, 95.25Kgs) and I have remained 3lb below or above that number ever since. I was a 58" waist and now a 34", I was an 8XL and now I'm a Large. I've lost over half my starting body weight -15st 4lbs (-217lbs, -98.4Kgs).

I'm addicted to food and I have learned that there is a FOOD MONSTER that lives inside mine and many other people's head, all my life it has controlled me and over the last 3 years I have trained to keep him in his cage and WHEN for one meal (Remember he is trained now), I let him out of his cage I can get him back in with very little issues. The FOOD MONSTER will be with me for the rest of my life as he is part of me.

I had a fight with a food monster and WON!!!! With no surgery or gym – This Manual is here to help you do the same.

I'm no nutritionist, Doctor Psychologist or scientist, I'm just a dad of 3 children, a husband, a normal person – I'm just like YOU, but who has lost over half his body weight and wants to help as many people as I can to lose weight.

Mine and my family's life is very different now – the physical journey has been huge, the psychological journey is 4 times bigger and a MASSIVE different journey that people don't see, understand or talk about at present – this is going to change!!!! – it's GOT TO!!!!

Anyway, enough about me!!!

HERE We Go!!!!

Oh, before we start – take your phone and get someone to take a full-length photo of you standing up – I would stay take one from a reflection in a full-length mirror, but it is highly likely you haven't got one in your house, because I didn't, but we will come on to that later.

ANYWAY - TAKE THE PIC – YOU ARE GOING TO NEED IT!!!

1. **THE FOOD MONSTER / the inner voice in your head.**

The food monster lives within all of us and a lot of people live in harmony with them.

There is a number of different FOOD MONSTERS, some focus on one thing like Cheese, crisps, biscuit, chocolate etc, etc – those monsters have an impact on our weight.

Others FOOD MONSTERS that make you feel guilt for eating food the wrong foods or too much food, and make you do things that are not good for your physical or psychological healthy – making yourself sick.

What I call a full-blown FOOD MONSTER hunts for everything edible and they are a whole different beast to tame, deal with and control, and will make you over-weight etc, etc. – this is the bad boy I've got!!!!

So here comes the imagination part that you need to start using.

This monster inside your head, now nothing dark and horrible, The FOOD MONSTER is a naughty, playful, mischievous, ugly, annoying, controlling, manipulative little ******* – you get the idea you need to picture it in your head – it helps believe me.

Right now we have all seen at 1 time in our lives a comedy sketch of someone chasing a chicken to try and get it back in their cage – well this is exactly what it is going to be like to get your food monster in its cage – the BAD news is its hard work and can take days – the GOOD news is it gets easier the more you train and control it.

So have you got an image in your head, again nothing dark or horrible – that won't help???? – if not you need to give this some thought as it is key to moving forward – put the manual down if you have to create the image as it is important as you are going to be living with them for the rest of your life and it is 1 of the keys to where you want to be.

Ok, living with the food monster is like living with a certain superhero inside you – bear with me, he turns green and you wouldn't like him when he's angry!!!! We all know that that guy changes when he is hurt or angry – your food monster does the same sort of thing, you know what makes you start over-eating everything in sight and the wrong food and the best way to manage him is to plan, avoid agitating or control him / her when they play up.

Ok the aim is - to have that food monster trained and getting in and out of its cage with very light issues and this is what we are going to train to do and achieve with different coping and managing techniques.

So, like training a dog this takes time – you can't just go to 1 class and it is trained, if only it was that simple. You must keep training the monster controlling the monster, like everything the more you do it the easier it becomes.

Controlled Let Outs – Remember the aim is to live in harmony with it!!!

This is where you focus and plan letting the FOOD MONSTER out. I would recommend that you keep it cage for quite some time before you do this. Before letting it out you must **PLAN, PLAN, PLAN – FOCUS, FOCUS, FOCUS** – and above all **LEARN FROM IT.**
You have to let the monster out sometime. But the key is you control it, not vice versa.
Tell the people that you are with what you are going to do and get them in on the plan, they should support you. If they don't you can plan for them not being on board!!!!

Break Outs – you need to be ready for break outs

Break outs can take you by surprise or creep up on you and need to be dealt with **FASTER THE BETTER**, like anything the more you do it the better you become. The biggest thing from dealing with a FOOD MONSTER break out is each time reduce the time it takes you to deal with the situation and **LEARN FROM IT** what worked well and what didn't – don't beat yourself up about it, it happens. Get the FOOD MONSTER back in its cage as soon as possible.

Have a break out containment plan

Food Monster Trap – Don't believe them – there lying

Monster traps are when you start think things that are negative like giving up, I'm ill because I've lost weight – 1 that a lot of people have is "I get to a certain weight loss and I think I've lost enough and then I go back and put the weight back on", mine was the 2 stone (28lb, 12.7kgs) – **ALL COMPLETE FOOD MONSTER TRAPS** – Food monsters will try anything in the book to try and get their own way. This often leads to what I call a punch through moment, this is where you just HAVE to push forward and break through that barrier – tell yourself it is a FOOD MONSTER TRAP – you will know when it is time to stop when you get to your final Golden numbers. You will get to know you own FOOD MONSTER TRAPS.

Contain the monster – Crack ON!!!!

When I started my weight loss journey, if the food monster got out, or was let out, it would take me 3 days to get him back in his cage, the damage was huge, and it was really hard work. But now I have him so well trained I can let him out and he does what I tell him most of the time – when he doesn't I use the other technique in this manual to regain control of him, quickly.

Onwards and downwards to the other techniques.

2. The 5cs.

During your wait lost journey, you are going to need to do all 5 of these or it is not going to work for the long-term Head and Maintain game – don't be scared, remember it takes time and practise.

I Follow What I Call The 5Cs – Change – Commitment – Challenge – Control – Consistent

Change – you are going to change your physical appearance with weight loss, you don't need to be a genius to work this out, but you also need to change mentally, if not you will go back or what I call "bounce", that is hit your target and then start gaining weight again. So firstly, don't uses the word target, use the words "golden numbers". A target suggests the you have finished – unfortunately you are never finished, it doesn't work like that because that FOOD MONSTER is just waiting for you to let your guard down.

Change Nothing, Nothing Changes

(FOOD MONSTER TRAP) + (BREAK OUT)

Commitment – Everything in life that needs to be done takes commitment whether that is time, head space, money, etc. But the biggest commitment you need is head space and time. The more commitment you give to yourself the better your weight lost journey will be. This will also be to exercise further into your journey, but don't panic – All I did was walking.

NEVER EVER EVER GIVE UP!!!!!

Challenge – WOW this is a big 1 on lots of levels, first of all the HEAD GAME challenge to get to the start of the physical challenge.

So let's focus on the HEAD GAME challenge, you need to figure out what makes you tick – you need to be completely honest with yourself and look at what you are good and the bad at. Now here is the tricky bit, you need to focus on the bad because they are the bits that is the biggest risk to mess your head up, you NEED to manage them and in an ideal world turn them in to positives. But we don't live in ideal world, if we did I'd have a six pack and be a multi billionaire.

So Managing them is just fine, to start managing them you need to know what they are so be honest with yourself and then come up with a plan to manage then because if you change nothing, nothing changes – 1 of the 3 Ps. (Please see below)

The Physical challenge is the easier part, as you lose weight you want to be more active and it needs to follow in as it is not just about food. Like I said, "all I did was walk", I did **NO** gym and just MOVED MORE.

Control – this is all linked to the FOOD MONSTER, you need to control it. Short but not simple, unfortunately!!!! You need to learn to control your thoughts and feelings and the reasons you eat too much food.

Consistent – You need to fine a consistent daily and weekly rhythm which is healthy and balanced and gives you weight loss, what you want to do is up to you. I help to break it down to daily and weekly routines. (What I did is in section 10)

There is so much information out there about what to eat, how to eat it, where to eat it, bluh bluh bluh………………. my advice is keep it simple and cook from scratch we didn't have large cave men / women.

The 3Ps - PLAN + POSITIVE MENTAL THINKING = POWER

PLAN your food, Always THINK POSITIVELY, which gives you POWER over the food monster

Ok enough Ps and Cs and all that – Onwards And Downward.

3. **Addiction.**

I am addicted to food, no question about it!!! – not any particular food, just food – **A FULL BLOWN FOOD MONSTER.**

Like any addiction you think about it all your waking minutes, when is your next meal, you're eating breakfast and thinking of lunch or even earlier – firstly you're not the only person that thinks like that – there are millions of people across the world that think like this – they just don't talk about it – WE are going to change that, please speak to someone about it – IT REALLY DOES HELP – is a massive start to controlling / beating all the types of FOOD MONSTERS.

I spoke many many times with a friend of mine, who is also a 28-year dry alcoholic (Huge respect) – I met him 8 years ago. We have had lots of conversations over the years, him talking about alcohol and me in the last 3 years talking about food and if you were to listen to our conversations and took out the 2 key words of FOOD and ALCOHOL you would think we were talking about the same thing – WE are ADDICTS!!!

The only difference with a food addictions is that with all the other big addiction you never have to put that in to your body or do it ever again if you don't want to – easier said than done I know!!!!

BUT with food you can't do that as obviously you will die, so you have to put some of what you are addicted to into your body for the rest of your life and that in my opinion is even harder - **BUT CAN BE DONE!!!!!!**

So we have to develop coping strategies for dealing with the Addiction and the cravings that go with it – the more you learn to train and control the food monster the easier your addiction becomes – It isn't easy and it takes practise and the 5Cs and 3Ps.

Remember you will know or will learn what makes your food monster angry, agitated and really rattles its cage. You have 2 choices
1) Don't upset it or tease it. (Which is hard when food is all around us)
2) Control it and show them who the boss is!!!!

Both are hard to do, both need practise and training to do.
I would say that a combination of the 2 makes is the best strategy for an enjoyable life and to get to living in as much harmony as possible with the Food Monster.

Addiction Transfer – you need to be aware of this bad boy when you control an addiction you can and probably will transfer it to something else. Now this doesn't have to be a bad thing, I have been addicted to and collected loads of things, for example: -

Keyring, Rubbers/erasers, Cookies jars (with no cookies), Uplighter lamps, Car trailers, Cars, Electronics, Coffee tables, Coats, Work.

And many many more, it would change, and I would never choose what it was or control what it was.

Or you give up smoking and you put on weight – Addiction transfer.

During my journey I started to understand how I worked, what made me tick and I was talking to a mother of 2 children I meet and she was saying I have Johnny and he is 16 years old and weighs 19st (266lbs, 120kgs) and I have Amanda who was as big as Johnny and now she lost the weight and now she is anorexic, she said she didn't understand it!!!! – I sat there and completely understood it – Amanda had addiction transferred and gone from 1 end of the scale to the other.

Did it worry me? – no because I listen and started to plan, I'm not going down that road!!!

Did I get addicted to weight loss – honestly yes, but the difference is I control it, not the other way around!!!! – today I'm with in Golden Number range

Am I Psychologist? – no I'm not – I just watch, listen and talked to people all my life and feel feelings and reflect.

Habit – Vulnerable Time.

This is an event that can be a time of day like getting in from work or sitting in front of the TV, somewhere that you are 1) at your most vulnerable and 2) you associate some certain foods. For example – going to the cinema and having popcorn or having a cake when you get in from work.

These habits / vulnerable times need to be focused on and changed to healthy substitutes, like taking grapes to the cinema – having something that replaces the same physical action / motion to eat helps to combat the habit – it worked for me. Always **PLAN, PLAN, PLAN.**

If you have a time of day that you are more vulnerable to eat non-healthy foods, or you are so hungry that you want to grab the easiest food. The best option is to 1) Admit it 2) **PLAN, PLAN, PLAN** 3) Have healthy food to grab.

4. **Keep It Visual.**

Reason for **KEEP IT VISUAL** – I never really focused on my actual size, the numbers meant nothing to me and still really don't it is just a guide for me and where I want to be. But in saying that you do need to absorb it!!! NOW remember that pic I told you to take well this is where this first comes in. Look at it……………………take as long as you like, hours or days if needed.

Ok now this photo of you is going to drive you on, but it is also going to be your before pic. So, get uses to it. The picture of The BIG Guy in the sofa, (section 14} which is me, I never knew that when my wife took that photo that it was going to change my life and thousands of other people's lives forever – Thank Mrs H xxx.

I had what I called my trophy belt this was an extremely large leather trousers belt that I had to keep my 58" waist trousers up and I just started making holes in it as my waist got smaller and smaller and the belt now goes around me over half way again. Every time I did the belt up during everyday it reminded me I was on a mission of "I'm losing weight today".

Now this is a big one Buy a full-length mirror, I didn't do this straight away. In my house with my wife and 2 x teenage daughter and growing up son we only had a what I call head and shoulders mirror – looking back that was just another way of me not having to see how big I'd become, now I love it!!!! When the girls are not hogging it!!!!!

FACEBOOK – Now I did my journey very publicly on my private Facebook page so all my friends could see and hopefully support me, which everyone did xx, but the reason I did it at the time was planning for the future of me being at the golden numbers that I wanted to be at, and WAIT FOR IT,………………………….HELP ME NOT TO GO BACK. I now have a Facebook group, but we will come on to that later.

This is a high-risk strategy because if I was ever to go back then the feeling and emotions (embarrassment, failure, etc) that I would feel and think would be not good. But I'm not going back so I don't need to worry about that – do it once, do it right. The decision is yours!!!!! – a lot of people that see me now usually say at some point – are you managing to maintain it then??? As if they expect people to put weight back on.

(I never knew it would go this public, but there you go, NEVER say NEVER)

There are many many other ways for keeping it visual, time for you to uses your imagination again – you can think of your own ways for keeping visual that work for you.

OH yeah!!!

Don't throw all your clothes away as you get smaller, keep 1 complete outfit in your largest size. Why? Because you can keep putting it on as you get smaller and it will keep it visual, plus when you hit your golden numbers you can take another full-length picture - it great fun!!!, but it reminds you of where you have come from.

5. **Head Game – Dreaming – Focus – Never Say Never – Never Ever Ever Give Up.**

Head Game this needs working on daily and everything in this manual links in together – can't stress enough if you choose not to follow some of the sections you will run into problems in what you know is a very hard journey.

Excuses – we are all very good at coming up with these, I'm a pro at it, but most of the time they are saying or thinking things like: -
It's not the right time.
I will do something when something happens.
I'm big boned.
If they don't like me for who I am you know what they can do.
I'm too big now to do anything about it.

A REALLY big one – I don't want loose / saggy skin.

Now, loose / saggy skin depends on how big you are and some about how old you are, and it is **NOT** as bad as you think.

The way I see it is you can't go to war and come back without scars, it makes you more unique, it reminds you of where you have been and come from. The way that I deal with it is to dress accordingly and I have, at times worn a man corset under my clothes for better shape – Shock – Horror – they are not just for women.

120% there is no way I would not have done the journey because of it!!

Your partner, I'm fairly sure that most of them would want you to be healthier, more active, be here longer, etc.

SO DON'T LET IT STOP YOU THERE ARE SO MANY MORE BENEFITS TO WEIGHT LOSS

Again, there is many many more, which I have probably said or thought most of them.

You might think that you don't have what it takes to lose weight, that you are rubbish at making the right choices when needed, that realising dreams are for other people, BUT I'll let you in to a little secret....... every person who succeeds will have times of doubt, times where they didn't think they had what it took and many occasions where they thought that their dream would never happen too!

What those who succeed do though is KEEP GOING, they work through the tough days / weeks / months and they dust themselves off and go again - that may need doing a number of times but if we keep doing it then dreams will come true - we are all worth more than we ever give ourselves credit for so please remember PERSEVERANCE OVER PERFECTION WILL WIN THIS BATTLE.

When I started My Journey I never in my wildest dreams thought that I would be where I am today.

This is how it was for me -

Dream

I started waking up in the morning around 38 years old, I'm now 43 and sit on the edge of the bed and look down and think "I'm still fat!!!!", now looking back and having time to think about it I have figured it out. In my dreams I was an average size man doing average activities and task, which in fact I could do not in real life. I don't know if I just thought / hoped that 1 day I would wake up thin – OH now there's a thing, I do wake up thin every morning now?!?!?! – 5 years later.

It was the 3Ps kicking in **PLAN – POSITIVE MENTAL THINKING – POWER –** just staying

Some people have asked me did or am I having a midlife crisis?!?!? – No, I'm having / had a midlife re-evaluation of my life – Crisis is out of control, I have worked my socks off to remain in control.

Focus

ME TIME - Ok here is a big one!!!!

All my life I have focused on other things, here are a few.

- Worked in the care sector since I was 17 years old – remember I became addicted to work.

- Thinking of others first – running around for them, doing things for them.
- Paying bills / mortgage, food etc.
- Providing for my family.

And many many more normal day life issues and events that we all face day in day out, BUT on a day to day basis in the top ten things to do that day I / ME never ever ever came onto the list – so there was never any time for ME.

Now that may sound like I'm saying to loses weight you need to be selfish – I'm NOT.

What I'm saying is that you need to give yourself time, space and energy to focus on you journey ahead. So, here's how I done it – top 10 jobs weight loss went to in the top 3. I give 120% effort to everything I do, I now save 10% for ME, just 10%. That means everybody else is still getting 110%, on a bad day and am only giving 100%, they still get 90% because come hell or high water I NEED 10% - it's not too much to ask?!?!?!

Punch Through Moments – are times in your journey were you need to just complete head down and go for it, it could be things like 1 of the barriers that you come up against in your head like "I've lost enough weight" when you haven't, or you are getting yoyo weighs up and down, up and down.

JUST KEEP GOING!!!!!!

SWITCH In My Head – I have installed a switch in my head and it has an ON/OFF switch so if I was off plan I visualise a switch in my head and turn it to on and I usually related that to a physically doing it by turning a key in a lock like my front door at home, once I'd turned it in the lock I was back on plan. So for example if you were going out and you decided/planned to be off plan, stay on plan till you leave the house to go out for the event. As you lock the door to your home, switch OFF eating plan – enjoy the evening - when you get home and unlock your home, switch ON eating plan – Crack On!!!

Never Say Never – NEVER EVER EVER GIVE UP

If you told me 5 years ago that I would lose just over half my body weight, be in national and international newspapers, websites and magazines and be sitting here in 2018 writing a manual about the psychological weight loss journey, I would have said,………………….. well I can't type want I would have said, you get the idea.

I climbed Snowdon mountain in 2017 with Mrs H and my son, I went on holiday abroad for the first time in 17 years and took our children for the first time, and I even done the more normal things like walked along the beach with my family that I soooooooooo long wanted to do, but never thought would happen.

All because I said things like "Never say Never"

- "I can do this"
- "I'm Losing Weight Today" (Please see section 7)
- "Do it once, do it right"
- "It's time to do this"
- "Never ever ever give up"
- "If it works keep doing it" – along as it is balanced and healthy"
- "Onwards and Downwards"

　　　　When things get hard – "Don't Give Up, Change It Up!!!!

Body Shape – KEEP GOING!!!!

As you lose weight your body shape changes, sometimes you think your stomach looks smaller and then sometimes you think your stomach etc looks bigger. This is because you can't control were your body loses weight so if you lose weight off your chest your stomach will look big and vice a versa. Sometimes an area of the body is the last place for the fat to come off – YOU HAVE JUST GOT TO KEEP GOING – IT WE ALL LEVEL OUT AT SOME POINT.

Don't compare your journey/weight loss to anyone else as we are all different.

Falling Off The Wagon – Don't Panic Or Feel Guilt

Eating something off plan, eating something you think you shouldn't – its not the end of the world. First of all don't feel guilt – you are human and its ok, but you do need to control or contain the **FOOD MONSTER** or it can really get out of control.

Something I also do is if I'm going to eat something off plan and that is going to affect my weight loss, I just pause for 5 seconds before putting in my mouth and think is this 120% worth eating it?!?!?!?.............. then if I put it in my mouth I would then think again is this worth it?!?!?!?................................

Basically, if you are going to eat it and affect your weight loss it must be ssssooooooo worth it if it isn't, DON'T EAT IT!!!!!!.........its your choice.

Draw a line under it as soon as you can, again the sooner the better and learn from each time it happens.

The more you learn to control and live in harmony with the FOOD MONSTER the easier it will become.

OR the best way to deal with having non – healthy food is to PLAN it, I don't mean each day or week, I mean special occasions!!! – Stick to the PLAN!!!!

It can be done – YOU can do it!!!

6. **Talk About It.**

Over the years, but especially in the last 3, I have spoken to a lot of people that are things like depressed, ashamed, at a loss, disgusted, don't know where to start with the weight issues / problem – whatever you want to call it – You can change it, start talking about it – WE have nothing to be ashamed and all the other negative words you can feel.

I enjoyed being big – probably the same as some of you reading this, and would think or say things like "I like being big", "I'll do something about it when I have to or something happens", "It is who I am and if they don't like tough" and many many more – said exactly the same, but here it is – unfortunately that has a direct impact on your life now and in the future and only you can unlock what works for you.

But talking about it with people that you know trust and love is the way forward to start the changing how you view yourself.

If we can get to talk about weight issues the way that people are starting to talk about mental health, we are getting on to the right lines.

7. I'm Losing Weight Today.

First thing, every single morning, I wake up I say to myself – **"I'm Losing Weight Today"** it must become like a heartbeat, it never stops!!!!!... it changes when you get to your golden numbers to, you've guessed it……………………………….. **"I'm Maintaining MY Weight Today"**

This is to help keep your weight loss in the top 5 things and sometimes higher, to do today and to keep it fresh in your mind – this really has worked for a number of people that have adopted this approach.

WANT weight loss MORE than food everyday

8. Weighing Regularly.

This is a 6-million-dollar question, and opinions vary, some say weekly, some say don't weigh go with look and others say weigh daily.

Every day is not healthy for your mind, weigh weekly a lot of people are told - If it is a consultant telling you - you pay them each week.

The other risk is you can find yourself eating to the scales, by this I mean you get on the scales and you have lost 2lbs from the day before so you think fantastic and you go down for breakfast as normal which is planned and then slowly through the day you eat things that you haven't planned for because in the back of your head you are thinking "I've got 2lb to play with and I'd be happy with a lb". (FOOD MONSTER TRAP)

Weighing every day, It is not unhealthy for your mind, only if you become obsessed with it. - Control

If you weigh every time you put something in or out of your body - that's unhealthy, boring and obsessional etc etc and you will crash!!!

Weighing once a day is focused, routine, consistent, rhythm controllable and measurable.

YOU ARE IN CONTROL - IT'S YOUR JOURNEY - DO WHAT YOU WANT!!!

Do what works for you keep doing it - don't let it control you, remember you control it!!! - If you don't want to weigh everyday don't, if you do then fill your boots - but just once a day maximum and try to keep it to the same time of day – first thing in the morning is best.

What I did???? – I weigh everyday – morning routine is – wake up put glasses on – have a pee - get naked - stand on scales - look at numbers – say I'm losing weight today – go and have planned breakfast ------------ I do this every single day as it keeps weight safe and were I want it to be.

Time – DON'T get obsessed with time, there is no quick fix – you go to fast your head will/can struggle to keep up – You can/will crash.

9. Weekly Rhythm.

My rhythm is weigh in Wednesday, relax Thursday, Friday, have some starchy carbs, in moderation. (I don't mean cheat day, I just mean relax because I got this,) Saturday start to drive onwards and downwards, Monday no starchy carbs what so ever and no sugary snacks, Tuesday, I have a what I call a physically light day, so if it is physically light only I will eat it. For example, chicken salad or soup, etc.

Wednesday Breakfast is a Banana, Lunch is a Yogurt and only have sips of drink from 1pm until I stand on the scales between 5.30pm and 6pm, soon as I get off have something to eat and drink that is on plan.

Wednesday is what I call my official weight day, but as I said in section 7 and 9, I weigh every day.

Exercise/move more needs to be part of your weekly rhythm to aid weight loss, like I've said start with lightly and build up from there.

Get in a weight loss rhythm – then hit the weekly repeat button – remember – healthy and balanced.

If You "Fall Off The Wagon" you need to contain the FOOD MONSTER as soon as possible and then damage limitation straight after containment.

10. Food And Exercise, Rhythm.

FOOD

Right food is number 10 on the contents page and a long way in to this manual – that is for a reason, the reason being is you lose weight in your head and not your stomach. All the other things in this manual are more important than food, but it obviously plays an important part too.

When I first started my journey in 2015, a very good friend of mine said "In your head this is done, you are just waiting for your body to catch up" – she was absolutely right!!!!

Biggest thing with your food is **PLAN PLAN PLAN PLAN**……………………. again, you get the idea!!!!!, some people find it helps to write it down.

Anyway – this is basically what I eat – low carb – low fat – low Sugar eating plan – **NOTE LOW NOT NONE**.

I mostly eat lean/all fat and skin removed meat, fish, it is baked or grilled with veg, fruit and salad. I also eat a maximum of 2 bananas a day. I do eat quite a bit of low fat, low sugar yoghurt daily. I add fruit to it, fresh, frozen and dried.

I do have tomato ketchup, mayo, salad cream etc all light, reduced fat or sugar and used sparingly.

I also eat 2 to 3 slices of wholemeal bread a day for fibre and drink 2 to 3 litres of fluid a day. If I have a sweet snack it is no more than 150 calories per day, this also includes crisps, biscuits, etc etc.

I have up to 330mls of skimmed milk a day or 40gs of cheese.

FAT – I put very little fat and oil into my body as to my thinking, why would I put that into my body if that is what we are trying to get out!!!!!

CARBS - I eat very little starchy carbs during my weight loss – only once or twice a week max and only 1 large cooking utensil spoon full. When I say starchy carbs I mean Potatoes, rice, pasta, beans and Lentils. THIS IS KEY TO MY WEIGHT SLOW – REDUCE STARCHY CARBS.

Everything needs to be in **MODERATION, HEATLHY** and **BALANCED – know what a normal portion looks like.**

If you are hungry, have a drink, if still hungry – eat – just not starchy CARBS.

KEEP IT SIMPLE

There is so much information out there about food – you need to find what works for you – but there are 3 things that remain the same no matter what you do: -
1. The Head Game and food monster remains the same.
2. If you put it in your body you need to burn it off.
3. Stick to what works – if it is healthy and balanced.

Exercise

Get yourself a device to count your steps that goes on your wrist, if you have a modern mobile phone there are a lot of free apps use the ones that uses GPS if going out for walk, they are the best.

The ONLY exercise I did was walking, NO GYM, at my biggest of 30st 4lbs (427lbs, 193.6kgs) I couldn't walk 300 metres without stopping for a rest and sit down. I started slowly to increase the distances every day and during weight loss would walk 10k to 20k steps per day. Maximum I've walked in a day is 21 miles (33.5KM).

Some people don't loses weight when they start exercise for the first week or 2, just keep doing it, it will pay off – your body just needs to get in to the new rhythm and you have to continue to be consistent – don't get disheartened.

You do what you want to do, you do need to do something, maybe not at the beginning but you will at some point – MOVE MORE, I call it. The more weight you lose the more you will want to do. Walking, cycling or swimming is a good place to start. By MOVE MORE I mean things like, in a shop take the stairs instead of the escalator, park further away from the supermarket, walk to the supermarket, wash the car instead of taking it to the car wash – keep it simple – MOVE MORE………… you get the idea.

You can use the full stomach feeling to focus yourself on exercising – so full stomach (with on plan food) = full fuel tank, you can "go for miles" have the feeling that you need / want to burn it off – use that feeling to increase your weight loss with good calorie burning exercise.
Be careful - If you think that you can over eat on high fat, high sugar, high calorie foods and then exercise them food off – **FOOD MONSTER TRAP.**

Little changes make HUGE differences!!!!

11. The Person You Are / Superpower.

Another **BIG** one, so here goes.

The person you are, let me try and explain, mine and my dad's first name is the same, don't ask me why? I think it was popular in the 70s. Anyway, he was known as BIG Tony and I was known as Little Tony. He was a big man at his heaviest being about 19st (266lbs, 120.6kgs). As I got older and taller and bigger, like most sons you want to grow up to be like you dad. Sure, enough I got the same nickname as him when I got in to my 20s both in age and weight. I absolutely loved being known as BIG Tony and all the banter that came with it, like "Tone, how many you reckon you could eat of them?" and "Do you remember the time you smashed that chair to bits?", because I was always surrounded by people that I liked and we supported each other. My size has never been a problem to me or anyone that mattered to me.

BUT, I couldn't go on forever at that size and I needed to change physically and mentally, but also hold on to and keep all the things that I love about myself and still have the physical presence and banter that being BIG Tony brings. Which is 1 of the hardest parts of the journey to navigate – but I DID IT!!!! – because I did all the things in this manual that I am talking about and I looked at what was important to me and how I could still achieve the same outcome with a different input – So what I mean is BIG Tony liked having a physical presence when being in a room, which you get at the weight that I was, Average Size Tony doesn't get that so I'm now known for my loud, floral shirts (Much to my children's dismay) – Same outcome different input – Happy days.

I'm Still Known As BIG Tony – WINNER

This banter / image who you are can be lots of things like how much beer you can drink, get the ball to BIG Tony he's like an OX, any many more – you are who you are, but you don't want them to be saying **"Do you remember BIG Tone, my word he could eat R.I.P"** – (that's a hard 1 to write) no sooner than they have to!!!

The other thing is the people that are around you, some of them will not take you seriously about your weight loss and will come up with comments/statements like these: -
"You have been on more diets than I've had hot dinners."
"1 naughty meal won't hurt"
"I love you no matter what size you are"
"Yeah yeah, I've heard it all before"
"I thought you were on a diet" – When you are just about to tuck into something that you have planned and looked forward for days or weeks.
There are many many more.

When you come up against a person like this, it depends on your relationship with them.

If they are a work colleague, someone down the pub or school, does their opinion really matter – NO
If they are friends or family that is a bit more difficult, I would explain to them that you are changing your lifestyle to look after yourself better and nothing is going to get in your way. This sometimes doesn't sink in the first, second or sometimes third and fourth times you tell them.

A lot of people don't or can't handle CHANGE (1 of the 5Cs) very well no matter how you go about it.

So, I found the best way is to show them and no matter what they say or do, you stick to your plan to lose weight.

THE MORE YOU LOSES THE MORE THEY TAKE YOU SERIOUSLY!!!!!

Something to remember is some people will be wanting things to remain the same for other reasons like: -
It makes THEM feel better and in control.
Scared of change, scared you are going to loses weight and leave them.
They have only ever known you as big.
To justify their own weight issues or lack of body confidence.
There are lots more, so when someone makes a comment or statement about your weight – THINK, "IS THAT PERSON IMPORTANT TO ME?" – if **they are then THINK ABOUT THE REASON THEY SAID IT?!?!?!?!**
Some people you have to reminded them you are still the same person inside as they can focus on the physical change and some people find it hard to except – this can make problems for you if not spotted and spoken about.
It is a difficult balancing act as you are going to change mentally as it is all part of the journey the key is to hold on to the parts of you that you love of yourself.
So, first talk to them, second SHOW them you are 100% serious and no matter what they say or do, YOU ARE LOSING WEIGHT. Surround yourself with positive thinking people, that you trust with open honest opinions. Obviously this easier said than done, but no one said this was going to be easy.

The Good News Is The More You Lose The Easier It Becomes

If you change nothing, nothing will change.

Superpower

Now this could sound complete nuts, up myself, etc, etc. but it is not, and it is part of your weight lost journey at some point.

So you start losing weight and everything is going well and then people start to notice. Then they keep noticing and then you see someone you haven't seen for a long time. They are even more blown away by the physical change and then the more you lose the more people start taking an interest and before long all you are talking about is weight lost – that's all fantastic. That is all physical which is, the easy part – new clothes, new hairdo, more energy, etc etc.

This is where the full-length mirror comes in that I spoke about right at the very beginning, because you will want to see yourself in a full-length mirror daily and you will want to take selfies and post on social media, enjoy it - I love it.

BUT what starts to get bigger and stronger in your head game is the EGO!!!! – now that needs controlling, if not it is going to cause a huge world of issues for you. (Now I'm not just talking about Men)

So here is where the superpower bit comes in, you are losing weight and feeling and looking great changing physically and going about your normal day life then you start to feel and think differently and feeling invincible, if I can do this I can do anything, like you have a superpower, which start to interfere with your normal day to day life. Your new acquired powers you need learn to control them, give yourself some thinking time, then enjoy them you really need to understand what is important in your life, as your journey will challenge this.
This happen to me, the EGO can be really hard to control, it is a very powerful thing. I have spoken to others that have lost weight and it happen to them to, the rule of thumb is the more you lose the bigger it becomes. Please be ready for when it comes along in your journey because it is highly likely it will. If you don't control it, it will create chaos!!!!!

I hope that makes sense to you and more importantly understand it – EGO is a hugely powerful thing, use it correctly.

Enjoy it – control it – use it – but please be careful

12. The Maintain Game.

YOU MADE IT TO YOUR GOLDEN NUMBER – HUGE WELL DONE

SO WHAT NOW??? DON'T PANIC!!!!

Remember this is never DONE, this is something you are going to have to monitor for the rest of your life, if not you will go back, what I call "Bounce" your weight will start to increase.

Change "I'm Losing Weight Today" to "I'm Maintaining MY Weight today"

So, give yourself 3lbs above and 3lbs below your "Golden Number" tweak your food slightly and slowly, but not much, introduce more carbs **slowly** – remember you eat it your body need to burn it. It is a balancing act.

What I did - I wanted to be 15st so I went down to 14st 11lbs and then recalibrate up from there and now float around 14st 11lbs and 15st most of the time. Remember the key is small changes, 1 at a time and it can take a few months.

You need to change from a weight loss rhythm to a maintain rhythm.

Remember I weigh every day, first thing in the morning so I can trim back when I need to. It's up to you when you weigh, just don't get obsessed.

When you get to this stage the way I see it is, We have worked far too hard to put weight back on and do it all again…………………………..********* that!!!!!!

Planning + Positive mental thinking = Power.

This can be pinch point, ONLY IF YOU LET IT, if you start to wobble **RE-READ THE MANUAL**, give yourself thinking spaces, focus on all the things that you have learnt about yourself during your weight loss journey – YOU KNOW WHAT WORKS FOR YOU – Focus on that picture I told you to take at the very beginning of this manual.

Don't let your guard down, because before you know it the FOOD MONSTER will be out and causing havoc for you.

DON'T CELEBRATE WITH FOOD, KEEP PLANNING YOUR FOOD, WITH SMALL SLOW TWEAKS – REMEMBER YOU HAVE WORKED TO DAMN HARD TO GO BACK!!!!! – GET INTO A MAINTAIN RHYTHM

DON'T LET YOUR GUARD DOWN - FOOD MONSTER TRAP!!!!!

13. On The Soap Box Moment!!!!

When **Government/People/Society** etc start looking at large people differently and stop judging them for the reasons etc etc etc that they are big **AND** Larger people start standing up and taking responsibility for themselves then we WILL kick the living daylights out of this international FOOD MONSTER Epidemic.

You can't think Oh we made smoking socially unacceptable, we can do it with large people. It doesn't work like that – you will make it worst!!!!! – trying to scare us won't work.

Healthcare Professionals – Now that is hard one, you are stuck in the middle, trying to help with the problem and the best way to fix it. Surgery is an option, it can deal with the physical side but not the psychological side and where there is a FOOD MONSTER they will 100% find away round that very expensive surgery to get the patient to continue to be overweight, as I'm sure you know, because of all the traits of a FOOD MONSTER and the addiction side of obesity (I hate that word) - More support is required in the psychology department of weight loss and if you start treating like an addiction, I think you will see better results.

The Weight Loss Sector – it needs to be about people not business (like a lot of things in this world) people are losing weight, but how many maintain and don't regain some, all or more weight? This is because you are focusing on FOOD to much and not the psychological side of weight loss.

FOOD, eating plans, diets, shakes, pills etc, etc, etc is easy to produce and sell and worth billions across the world!!!!! – Head space is not!!!!! – BUT IS KEY!!!!!!

It is **NOT** all about FOOD!!!!!! the people that need/want to lose weight are saturated with information ABOUT FOOD – the very thing WE struggle with or are addicted to!!!!! – REALLY!!!!! – it's like telling an alcoholic all about alcohol, we know!!!! – focus more on the psychological journey you are going to take people along – not just mainly FOOD – DO IT ONCE, DO IT RIGHT.

Or is it about repeat business?

Food/Weight loss Bloggers – you have been there, you should know. Then you lose loads of weight and spend most of your time posting pictures of food to people that struggle with food, doesn't matter it is healthy, low fat food, etc, etc its FOOD. You people should know, of all people, that only helps a very small amount. Start talking more about the psychological journey and how you did it to help people more.

The lovers and the haters (Keyboard Warriors) - you are both not helping – it needs to be balanced. You are just making it harder – move on.

Ps before you start I have worked full-time all my life a minimum of one job etc etc etc!!!

Celebrity Chefs – some of you are doing your bit for healthier food, thank you. There needs to be move healthy cooking going on producing low calorie/ low fat meals.

Everyone - is focusing on giving out FOOD/nutrition information it is not all about FOOD – We DON'T need so many pictures, facts and figures anymore.

Larger People/People That Want To Lose Weight - There is no fast fix, it takes years to get large it takes years to get to average size or where you want to be. It needs to take that long for you to change your lifestyle and your thinking.

It is time for every larger person whether it is 2st (28lbs, 12.7kgs), 3st (42lbs, 19.05kgs), 5st (70lbs, 31.75kgs), 7st (98lbs, 44.45kgs), 10st (140lbs, 63.50kgs)…………. you get the idea, to stand up and across the world to **take**

responsibility for themselves and stand together, because together we are stronger.

It is time for **CHANGE – IT IS TIME TO DO THIS!!!!** – to be here longer for ourselves and our loved ones.

Me – Now you could say that I'm writing this Manual to make money??? – and you may be right!!!
BUT MORE IMPORTANTLY I'm writing this manual to **help people lose weight and maintain it**, help me maintain my weight loss, to help change the weight loss sector.

Having been to the super big size side of life and managed to come back, me and others must hold some of the keys and information needed to help others in this global epidemic – Onwards And Downwards.

KICK THE LIVING DAYLIGHTS OUT OF AS MANY FOOD MONSTER AS I POSSIBLE CAN

PHEWWWWW!!!!! And breath – I think that covers everyone.

OH, there is one other thing – The BIGGEST THANK YOU TO each and every one of the people that I have come into contact within my life – a very small amount of you I can't stand, but you still brought things to the table of my life, which now helps me write this Manual.

14. The Big Guy.

The Big Guy as I said that the beginning of this manual The Big Guy in the 2 seater sofa is me and I have always loved that Guy because he is me and I don't regret being over 30st (400lbs or 181kgs) because if I hadn't of gone there then I wouldn't have been there to have learnt all these things that I've written in this manual and inspire and help so many people so far. Plus, it makes me more unique as not many people haven't been to the extremes of where I have and come back.

TO THE BIG GUY - We will never meet again but you will live on in social media, international media, my phones, photo albums, and in this manual, we will never meet again, but thank you and I love You Big Guy because you are me and you have changed so many lives already – Always be proud of who you are and what you have done.

If I can just help one person, to stop from going down the surgically route, health conditions better and to get to where they want to be with the Golden Numbers – **Then I / WE WIN THE WAR AGAINST THE FOOD MONSTER!!!!!**

If you want to catch up with me, I and many others will be food Monster fighting in – Facebook group – **FIGHTING THE FOOD MONSTER MANUAL** – Hopefully see you there.

I absolutely hate how I look in the picture on the left as much as I absolutely love how I look in the picture on the right.
But one thing remains the same in both and that is I love the person I am and obviously Mrs H and the children.

The picture of me on the left sitting on a 2-seater sofa I was 30st 4lbs (427lbs,193.6Kgs)

The picture on the right is the same 2-seater sofa at 15st (210lbs,95.25Kgs)

A loss of 15st 4lbs (217lbs, 98.4Kgs – IT CAN BE DONE

NEVER EVER EVER! GIVE UP.

WE TOGETHER CAN WIN THE WAR AGAINST THE FOOD MONSTERS

15. Notes To Self.

There is a huge amount of information in this manual, so I have created notes to self list for you. I have put a lot of the bullet points there for you but add your own – **IT'S YOUR LIFE – your FOOD MONSTER – YOUR WEIGHT LOSS JOURNEY – YOUR FUTURE!!!!!**

- NEVER say NEVER
- **DON'T LET FEAR OF LOOSE / SAGGY SKIN STOP YOU**
- You lose weight in your head, not your stomach.
- SPEAK TO SOMEONE ABOUT IT
- WANT weight loss MORE than food
- Monitor starchy CARBS – Eating less STARCHY CARBS is key.
- 3 Ps, - Plan, Positive mental thinking, Power.
- 5Cs – Change – Commitment – Challenge – Control – Consistent.
- Keep it simple.
- Keep 1 of your Largest size outfits – you will need it.
- Stay positive – Don't give up, change it up!!!
- Had a bad day - Onwards And Downwards.
- Be honest with yourself.
- Learn from it.
- Food Monster traps – spotting them is key.

Your FOOD MONSTER TRAPS: -

- Have a break out containment plan for the FOOD MONSTER

Your Containment plan: -

- Contain the monster – Crack ON!!!!

- If you put it in your body, you need to burn it off.
- Stick to what works – as long as healthy and balanced.
- Move More, little things make HUGE differences.
- REMEMBER THE EGO WILL COME – BE READY.

More notes to self: -

Printed in Great Britain
by Amazon